Glin Bayley

Healing after Heartbreak

Fifty days to take you from your
heartbreak to your heart song

R3THINK PRESS

First published in Great Britain in 2020 by
Rethink Press (www.rethinkpress.com)

This book is dedicated to you
and your healing journey. It takes
courage to embark on a journey
like this. I believe that if you have
this book in your hands you are
already one step closer, to not
only healing yourself, but towards
finding your joy again and living
a life you love.

Contents

Introduction   I

How to use this book   3

Day 1-50   6-104

The path forward   107

Acknowledgements   109

The Author   110

Introduction

Heartbreak comes in many different forms. Whether it is caused through the ending of a relationship, the loss of a loved one or a dream that has been shattered, the pain of heartbreak is very real.

It can be all-consuming and difficult to see a future beyond the heartbreak. The sense of feeling lost or stuck or numb can leave us wondering whether we can ever know true happiness again.

Right now, if you are experiencing heartbreak it can be hard to imagine what it is like to know true joy and to feel alive. There may be a part of you that is comfortable with this emptiness; you may not feel up to doing anything. That's OK.

But if there is another part of you that wants to access the feeling of being alive and being happy then this book will help you on your path.

When my marriage ended in 2014, I never thought I'd feel joy in my heart again. I was lost, I didn't know who I was outside of my marriage and I felt that the best part of my life was over.

Through my own healing I realised that this wasn't the truth and I could find a love that was unconditional and true, one that I could trust would never leave my side. That unconditional love I discovered came from myself to myself and in receiving it I transformed my life.

I manifested a new life in Australia, I moved from England and started over. I manifested new friendships and relationships that helped me grow from strength to strength, I discovered my creative side and as a result I manifested a new career aligned to my heart which led to me to start my own business and leave my corporate role behind.

My life today couldn't look more different to the one I was living in 2014, and the joy I feel within my heart isn't anything I could have imagined for myself when I was in my heartbreak.

In seeing my own transformation, I wanted to share in this book the poems and healings that have helped take me from my heartbreak to my heart song.

I have one wish for you, and that is transformation of your life to your own heart song – where you discover your deepest joy and look back with a real knowing that life is always working for you.

How to use this book

There are fifty poems and fifty healings in this book, and the intention is that it will take you fifty days to complete your healing process.

Read the poem for each day and complete the daily healings with diligence and discipline. In seven weeks, it is my hope that you will have discovered your heart song.

This healing journey will require a lot from you and needs your firm commitment to stay the course.

Many of the healings demand deep reflection and self-exploration; you may find the discipline required to complete this process challenging.

If you are committed to getting to know who you are and living a life you love it's a journey worth taking.

It starts with a choice: to stay where you are and in your heartbreak or transform your life.

The choice is yours.

So, don't delay your healing: start today. This is your journey to your heart song, and you won't be looking back for long when you see what treasures lie in front of you.

Heartbreak

Today's date:

Heart Song

Fifty days from today the date will be:

Day 1

A new dawn
A new day
Today's the day
I find my way

I search in earnest
For the truth that is me
Beguiled by life's beauty
As I learn to be

My heart is open
Roaming wild and free
The truth I am seeking
Is in all that I see

My light has been off
But now it shines bright
With no fear of the darkness
I welcome the night

Dear one, you are here because your heart has been broken and you are in pain. At this moment it may feel as though you will never be happy again. It hurts like hell and you feel deeply the loss for all that you had and the future you had envisaged.

You have no idea right now how you will get through this, and a huge part of you wants to close your heart down so you can never hurt like this again.

I urge you, dear one, please don't close your heart. Let me take you from your heartbreak to your heart song. Let me show you how to heal yourself and become open to receiving an unconditional love that you will never lose.

HEALING 1 – Buy yourself a beautiful notebook to begin your journal. Choose one that makes you smile and begin a daily practice of gratitude. It has been proven that misery and gratitude cannot co-exist, so it is time to eliminate the misery that you are feeling. Each day, for the next fifty days, choose a minimum of three things to be grateful for and write them down.

By the time you finish this healing journey you won't have to take my word for it, you'll have solid evidence of how profound the results are when you practise daily gratitude.

Day 2

Sometimes I wonder
What happens next
When life's a little confusing
It's time for my specs

I see a little more clearly
The closer I look
I don't have all the answers
As I write my life book

Into the wild I go
Fighting my fears of being alone
Giving myself courage
To stand tall on my own

Life is not easy
But it's a precious gift each day
So I love myself dearly
As I work to find my way

Life is uncertain, dear one, and at times of heartbreak it is particularly daunting. Building the courage to stand tall on your own can be scary, but the rewards that come when you do are incredibly fulfilling.

When you discover the courage to stand tall, you'll be unstoppable and all that you want will become available to you, but for this to be true you must begin with cultivating a deep self-love.

Without a deep self-love you will always be vulnerable to the actions and thoughts of others. This will weaken your spirit over time.

With a deep inner love you will be able to move forward with a knowing that regardless of how many times you stumble you have the strength to get back up after each and every fall.

HEALING 2 – Deepen your self-love by writing a list of all of the qualities you love about yourself. Once you have this list, read it out loud to yourself in front of a mirror – looking into your eyes – twice a day.

When you see yourself sincerely sharing all that you love about yourself as you look deep into your eyes, what you allow yourself to see are the same eyes and face that others will see when you tell them all the things you love about them.

If what you see doesn't look and feel sincere, then you know that you have work to do. Continue this exercise until you really believe the person you are looking at in the mirror.

Let yourself feel the qualities you describe to know they are true.

Day 3

Have the courage
To step outside
Take a deep breath
Your direction you decide

A small step first
Then another
Follow your heart
What will you discover

Little by little
One travels far
Courage my friend
To be who you are

Brave the wilderness
What will you find
That your home is in front
And not behind

Sometimes with heartbreak, dear one, we experience a loss of direction. We had a vision of the future that no longer looks the same as the one we envisaged.

This can be deeply unsettling and it's normal not to know what we should do next when we are feeling the pain of loss.

The message here is that you have to make a decision to step outside and choose a direction. Standing still isn't an option; the longer you stand still the further you are from the future you want.

HEALING 3 – Make a list of all of the things you've wanted to do in your life but haven't so far. Fill a whole page if you can, pick three from your list and choose one thing you could do for each of them that would move you closer to achieving them.

Start by taking one small step today and when you are ready take another. It will show you that you can go a long way just by taking small steps – be brave enough to take that first step.

Remember your future is in front of you, not behind you. You won't feel lost once you decide to take that first step.

Every new journey begins with a first step, choose yours today.

Remember to write down the three things you are grateful for and remind yourself twice daily in front of the mirror of your great qualities.

Day 4

Believing in yourself
It's so easy to say
I find myself drifting
As I find my way

Stopping to listen
Seeking the stillness within
The voices consume me
As I seek to begin

A new life awaits me
Of peace and inner quiet
I watch the world around me
As it continues to riot

I pause and connect
With the truth that is me
Trusting my journey
Will always set me free

Embarking on a new chapter isn't easy and it's OK, dear one, if you find yourself drifting aimlessly at times. If you do, firstly, it's important to not judge yourself for where you are.

Secondly, it's time to pause and connect to the truth within you. Each of us has an inner guidance system, but it's easy to forget to tune into it.

Know that it is there and that it is designed to guide you. You can begin to access it by becoming still and being open to listening for what it is telling you.

HEALING 4 – Dedicate 5 to 10 minutes every day to meditation. Quietening your mind allows you to access your intuition. Set a timer, close your eyes and be still. Initially you may find it hard to control your thoughts. If this is the case, focus your attention on your breathing.

When your thoughts run over and over in your mind it's difficult to hear your inner guidance system. Becoming still through meditation allows those thoughts and voices in your head to subside and gives you the space needed to hear the truth within you.

After one full week of meditation practice – Think what your intuition is telling you about the future direction of your life and write down your interpretation. If it's easier, jot down a few notes about what you feel after each session and see what emerges.

Keep up this practice along with listing your daily gratitudes and your self-love mirror exercise for the remainder of the fifty days – note in your journal what you learn and hear from your inner guide.

Day 5

Laughing lots
Being goofy with your smile
Your sides splitting
You'll be aching awhile

The pain is good
As the reminder is clear
That laughing saves lives
Of ones you hold dear

The gift of you
Is your humour today
Laughter fills the air
As you come out to play

One of the things you may have forgotten, dear one, while navigating your heartbreak is what it means to laugh and have fun.

Laughing is a great healing process because it sets off a chain reaction in the body that promotes physical and psychological health. Laughter lowers your body's cortisol levels (stress hormone) and relieves emotional tension.

Laughing helps you let go of negativity and also makes it much easier to combat your fears and overcome adversity.

HEALING 5 – Introduce a daily dose of laughter, especially when you don't feel like it. Find a video clip, a movie or comedy show to watch that makes you laugh or share a meme or joke with a friend and make them laugh too.

Laughter is a wonderful gift to share with others, it's contagious and spreads happiness. At moments of sadness try to use laughter to connect with people.

Also, remember, if you are able to laugh at the small things it will make it much easier to laugh off the big things.

Laughter eases pain: don't miss the chance to indulge in it and share that gift today.

Daily reminder

- ♥ Three gratitudes
- ♥ Self-love into the mirror twice daily
- ♥ Meditation
- ♥ Laughter

Day 6

Live spontaneously
Love without condition
Be true to your soul
Make happiness your mission

Give all that you are
No half measures
To see life's beauty
And all its treasures

Fear is an illusion
Don't let it get in the way
You are enough as you are
So remember that today

Heartbreak can lead us to forget how much wonder there is in the world and how many beautiful things surround us every day.

Fear often takes over because of the uncertainty of this new world; what once seemed exciting and adventurous can now feel scary and daunting to undertake on your own.

When you love yourself without condition there is a freedom that comes with it. A freedom to accept a life where you are more than enough just as you are. One where you can adventure by yourself because it proves to you that your own company is valued and to be treasured.

HEALING 6 – Choose an activity to do by yourself, either book a weekend away or plan a day trip some-where new. This is your time to live spontaneously to show yourself that you are more than enough. You can appreciate life's beauty without someone else to validate it.

Trust that time by yourself will allow you to learn more about what you appreciate about the world around you and also give you the opportunity to recognise how you can live true to your heart.

While you adventure, notice all the ways in which being in your own company fuels your energy levels and jot these down. Make sure to write your notes up in your journal. Capture your memories with a postcard of the place or print out a selfie to include in your journal.

Daily reminder

- ♥ Three gratitudes
- ♥ Self-love into the mirror
- ♥ Meditation
- ♥ Laughter

Day 7

P ower up lovely
  Don't be afraid
Follow the breadcrumbs
On the new path laid

Pay attention now
There is much to learn
You've got what it takes
So don't fear the burn

Keep moving forward
Momentum is key
You'll discover you are closer
To where you want to be

Don't stop now
You have everything to gain
The journey may be tough
But it's so worth the pain

Moving on from heartbreak isn't easy, dear one, and the journey can be painful. It's through the pain and from your heart being broken open that your biggest growth comes.

It might not always seem this way, but trust that there is so much you can gain from this experience.

Your path ahead is leaving breadcrumbs for you to follow, but you will only see them if you look forward not back.

HEALING 7 – Write a letter to yourself from your future self, dated three months from now. What guidance would your future wiser self be sharing with you and what encouragement would your future self be giving you? Seal the letter to be opened in three months' time and find out how much wisdom your future self actually has.

We know what we need to hear better than anyone else, but we don't often allow ourselves the chance to voice these kind, generous words.

When you open this letter in three months' time notice the bread-crumbs that revealed themselves to you along the path that your inner intuition was guiding you towards. You'll probably find that it knew all along what you needed; let your current self hear from your future self.

You might choose to repeat this exercise every quarter and see how good you are at guiding your life – you know more than you think.

Daily reminder

- ♥ Three gratitudes
- ♥ Self-love into the mirror
- ♥ Meditation
- ♥ Laughter

Day 8

B eauty lies in the eyes of the beholder
It's in all that surrounds us
and never gets older

Breathe it in, the magic of your day
Giving thanks for the miracles
You enjoy along your way

Pausing for a moment to take it all in
Knowing we don't get long here
And so we must begin

Seeing it all clearly, as it's meant to be
Loving everything in humanity
For all of eternity

If you're seeking to get to your destination, dear one, the one where you no longer feel the pain, it's natural to wish time away.

But know that by doing this we are rejecting our one precious life. It may not be easy for you to see how beautiful it is right at this moment but know that every moment of your life counts.

HEALING 8 – Take time to pause and notice all the beauty that exists in the world around you. Notice the perfection of nature and acknowledge how the seasons play a role in the evolution of life. Acknowledge the season you are in now and make a short note of what this season means to you and what you think it is teaching you.

This may be a season in your life you just want to get through but see it clearly and understand that it has its place in your life.

There is much we can learn from nature and from recognising that we don't always see what's going on underneath the ground, but we can trust there is growth even though the green shoots aren't visible yet.

Trust in what you are planting through this healing process, you'll reap the rewards of what you sow.

Daily reminder
- ♥ Three gratitudes
- ♥ Self-love into the mirror
- ♥ Meditation
- ♥ Laughter

Day 9

Dream big
Take some chances
Have hope
No backward glances

Look within
Find who you are
Trust yourself
And you'll go far

Believe always
The path will clear
Greatness awaits
No time for fear

Give others
The gift of you
Your uniqueness
Is your value true

When we are rediscovering our own path after heartbreak, it can sometimes be difficult to trust ourselves to know what to do next.

But the truth is the answer, and it is always available to you if you allow yourself to hear it, dear one. Sometimes it requires feedback from those who know you best.

HEALING 9 – Ask those who you have a trusted relationship with, and those who love you, to share examples of what they can always count on you for. Ask a minimum of five people to provide two examples each.

When you see what others can count on you for you will start to see the strength of your character. In knowing your strengths, you can build a clearer understanding of how you can apply those strengths to your circumstances and move forward with confidence.

When you ask the people you trust for feedback, you have to make a decision to truly listen and accept the gift they are giving you. Honour their gift by accepting and acknowledging the strengths they see in you.

Accept – do not reject the gifts they give you.

Daily reminder
- ♥ Three gratitudes
- ♥ Self-love into the mirror
- ♥ Meditation
- ♥ Laughter

Day 10

Your legacy
What will it be
Your purpose
What do you see

Look within
Follow your heart
Be brave
Make that start

Go forth
Have an impact
Helping others
Success you'll attract

Your legacy
What will it be
Your gift
To set others free

Your purpose
What do you see
Being true
To your own destiny

When we lose someone we love, dear one, what we are left with is their legacy imprinted in our hearts: the love we once received and the meaning we made from the times we had together.

While you may be feeling the full effects of heartbreak and loss, please know that you will have left a legacy imprinted in their heart too, even though you may not always get the opportunity to fully appreciate your impact on them.

Knowing that others have an impact on us and we have an impact on others, it's important to understand that we can *choose* how this legacy represents us and what difference we wish to make.

HEALING 10 – Consciously consider and write down what impact/imprint you wish to leave on others. Are you currently interacting with others in alignment with your desired impact? What actions would you need to take to move you closer?

What's important in doing this healing is not to judge yourself for your imperfections but realise that you can choose how you want to make others feel after an interaction with you.

Begin to live the legacy you want to leave: it's a gift you can give to others, and it also helps you to see the impact you can make.

Daily reminder

- ♥ Three gratitudes
- ♥ Self-love into the mirror
- ♥ Meditation
- ♥ Laughter

Day 11

G ive people the gift of you
The beauty of your smile
Your love so true

Honour who you are
The essence of your soul
Our world deserves to see
Your brilliance unfold

Your value to others
Is your true story shared
Unleash your power
As your heart is bared

When we are hurting, dear one, it's natural for us to see only the sadness in our life story, but the truth is that there is so much richness that we bury with our pain.

Each one of us has a beautiful story inside. One that would help others to learn and heal their lives. Stories are incredibly powerful and sharing them is how we have always passed on knowledge from one generation to the next.

Sharing our personal stories helps people learn more about us, builds deeper connections and helps us to realise that we are not alone when it comes to navigating difficult challenges in our lives.

HEALING 11 – Write down your personal story, the story of your life so far; speak it straight from your heart. Set a timer for exactly 10 minutes and see how much you can get down on paper. This exercise works best when you handwrite rather than type. Do not edit your story or overthink as you write, it's healing when you let it flow from within.

As you read your story back, please read it as though you were reading someone else's story for the first time. What did you learn about this person and how moved were you by their life journey?

Look for what inspires you and see how anchoring your thoughts in this narrative will help you to help yourself and others through sharing experiences.

Daily reminder
- ♥ Three gratitudes
- ♥ Self-love into the mirror
- ♥ Meditation
- ♥ Laughter

Day 12

I chose me today
To be wild and free
The fear of judgement
I will no longer see

Today I called time
I acknowledged my worth
My heart certain
Of my value on earth

You may not see it
And that I understand
But I'm worth no less
Though you misunderstand

Oh, how I love me
My heart expands
Accepting my truth
As my soul demands

Heartbreak can be experienced in so many ways, dear one. Sometimes the hurt from that heartbreak can lead us to being less than generous in our judgements about who we are and how we see ourselves.

To free yourself from the pain of heartbreak, it's necessary to see that the loss of someone or something in your life does not diminish your worth or make you someone of less value.

Without acknowledging this truth, you limit your ability to grow. By being less than generous with yourself about the truth of your own value means that others lose out on all that you have to give.

HEALING 12 – It's time to demonstrate that you are choosing yourself. It could be a simple thing like playing your favourite song and dancing around the room or it could be buying yourself some beautiful flowers or booking yourself a pampering treat.

When we show ourselves small acts of kindness, we reinforce the value we see in ourselves. The more we act with intention to love and choose ourselves, the more we acknowledge the truth of who we are.

Believing your own value will free you from the need to have others see it. The magic that happens when you see your own value is that others then see it too.

Daily reminder

- ♥ Three gratitudes
- ♥ Self-love into the mirror
- ♥ Meditation
- ♥ Laughter

Day 13

The magic of happy
Making you smile
Those gloomy thoughts
Disappear awhile

Happiness a choice
Always within
Must you deny it
Your heels dig in

Let go
And let things be
Be happy
For all to see

You see it's contagious
And spreads like fire
Your impact is greater
Than your deepest desire

We all know that happiness is ultimately a choice, but heartbreak often leaves us feeling that it's an impossible place to reach.

It seems strange to say, but sometimes it can be easier to stick with the feelings of sadness, however painful, than actively choose happiness for ourselves. It's worth taking a moment, dear one, to acknowledge whether you've noticed any patterns emerging of you denying opportunities to be happy.

This could be turning down offers of help, not responding to invitations from friends or family to connect, or actively choosing activities that continue to remind us of what we have lost.

HEALING 13 – Today's healing is going to require you to switch your focus from yourself to someone else you care about. Ask them about what makes them smile and consider how you could contribute to making them smile today. Make a note in your journal about what you felt when you consciously focused on putting a smile on someone else's face.

When we see that we have the ability to put a smile on someone's face, we see the power we each have to make the world a happier place. Heartbreak can make our own world seem dark but taking action to make others smile is a small step in showing that we don't need to let it define our lives.

Daily reminder

- ♥ Three gratitudes
- ♥ Self-love into the mirror
- ♥ Meditation
- ♥ Laughter

Day 14

D o you have
The disease to please
Even though it hurts
And you are on your knees

Putting others first
So you come last
Doing your best
But failing fast

Are you honest
With what you need
Expressing your truth
So you are freed

In service of others
You are admired
But the more you give
The more is required

Self-service
Is necessary too
Don't feel guilty
For choosing you

Nobody wants to experience heartbreak. It can be one of the most painful experiences we go through in our lives. However, the desire to avoid heartbreak means that we sometimes find ourselves in a position where we are trying to please everybody.

We know deep down that we aren't being true to ourselves, but our fear of rejection can leave us feeling that we have no choice but to please others as a means to keeping them in our lives or being accepted by them.

Often, not expressing what we feel creates more and more frustration and inner angst, further diminishing our sense of self. This makes it ever harder for us to remain authentic to who we truly are and be accepted for ourselves.

HEALING 14 – Today's healing requires you to do a relationship audit of the main people in your life. Write down the names of these people; they could be family, friends, work colleagues or other acquaintances you spend time with. Notice if there are people on your list who you feel you are not being your authentic self with.

Perhaps you have relationships with people who you feel on edge with, not free to be you. If that is the case, now is the time to consciously reduce how much time you spend in those relationships and focus more time on those with whom you can be yourself.

If we are to heal our heartbreak, we must be able to be the fullest expression of who we are. Unfortunately, this won't happen if we continue to invest time in trying to please the people with whom we feel we cannot be ourselves.

Daily reminder

- ♥ Three gratitudes
- ♥ Self-love into the mirror
- ♥ Meditation
- ♥ Laughter

Day 15

Trust your intuition
It knows you well
Your heart's desire
On what you dwell

Make a decision
What if you dared
A leap of faith
Though you're scared

Imagine a future
That you designed
The freedom of living
A life your heart defined

Take your first step
You know how
Don't delay anymore
Your time is now

Intuition is something we all have access to if we let ourselves acknowledge its existence.

We often have an inner knowing that can't easily be explained or rationalised by our five senses. This deeper sense of understanding and intelligence is only available to us when we silence our busy minds from thoughts and stories.

Intuition is a natural guide for making sense of the world around us. Those who are deeply connected to intuition are able to make clear decisions about their lives and move forward with confidence using this inner wisdom.

Our heart knows what is right for us, even if our mind can't rationalise how our heart knows this.

HEALING 15 – Today I'm reconnecting you to meditation if you haven't kept up with the daily practice suggested in Healing 4. Start paying attention to your inner guidance system by quietening your mind through a 10-minute meditation. Notice what is arising from your heart. What do you hear? What do you know to be true for you? What do you feel called to do today? Not out of fear but from a place of love. Take one small action today in alignment with what your heart's wisdom reveals through your meditation; one you don't have to question, just see what unfolds when you trust it enough to take action.

During times of heartbreak we can feel lost; finding ourselves doesn't appear easy. But our inner guidance system is ready to help us when we listen. It won't lead us astray, but we have to learn to trust and act without question from this place of inner knowing: this place where there is no fear.

Daily reminder

- ♥ Three gratitudes
- ♥ Self-love into the mirror
- ♥ Meditation
- ♥ Laughter

Day 16

She found her freedom
Won the fight
The internal struggle
To find the light

Her fire re-ignited
Flames burn clear
No stopping her now
Nothing to fear

She lost her way
But the truth she found
The love within
And all around

The beauty of her
Wild and free
Shining her light
As bright as can be

What we focus on we magnify, and what we think about we bring about.

When you are doing what you can to heal, dear one, it's not always easy to keep your thoughts focused on the life you want to create; it's only natural to direct your energy to the life you once had or the life you thought you were going to have.

When we continue to spend our time focusing on what we don't have, we increase the intensity of our struggles rather than invite new opportunities.

When we start to invest energy in creating the life we want, we begin to see the ripple effect across different areas of our lives, and we recognise how much power our thoughts and mindset have over the reality we experience.

HEALING 16 – Ask yourself where you want to be one year from now. What one thing would you like to be celebrating that you made the commitment to pursue today?

Choose something that inspires you and take one action towards it today, no matter how small. It might be something as simple as making a firm non-negotiable decision to move towards your dream – don't give up on the life you want, it's available to you if you keep moving forward. Make a note of the commitment you have made for yourself that you'd like to celebrate this time next year.

When you look back one year from now, you'll thank yourself for not giving up on you. Life hasn't unfolded as you'd wished, but know that it's made you stronger and more resilient so that you can achieve things you might never have tried had it not been for this heartbreak.

Daily reminder

- ♥ Three gratitudes
- ♥ Self-love into the mirror
- ♥ Meditation
- ♥ Laughter

Day 17

Dance around your living room
Sing loudly out of tune
Catch yourself in the moment
And laugh at being a loon!

Feel the lightness of freedom
The joy in your heart
From the energy of your love
When you let your fear depart

Don't let the voices steal
The smile on your face
Nor the sparkle in your eyes
And the life you embrace

Our greatest growth occurs in pain. The realisation that every single human on the planet will grow from an experience of heartbreak is a powerful way of acknowledging that our hearts need to break to become stronger – it's part of being human.

The hurt you have experienced, dear one, will strengthen your heart and you can decide how to use that new-found strength as a force for good.

Moving your body is a great way to release energy and shift your focus from what has been lost to what will be gained from this experience.

HEALING 17 – Remind yourself of what it feels like to be free and full of joy. Choose a song that makes you smile and want to move your feet. Move your body and dance like nobody is watching! Begin to see yourself in all the glory that is you – being you.

Acknowledge that your heart is growing strong and there is much to celebrate. Keep reminding yourself that heartbreak is part of our human experience, you are not alone.

Each time you begin to forget, play that song and dance.

Daily reminder

- ♥ Three gratitudes
- ♥ Self-love into the mirror
- ♥ Meditation
- ♥ Laughter

Day 18

The magic sauce
What is it you say
Making your fears
Just melt away

It's one we have
To access within
The sauce that inspires
A new life to begin

You may not know
Its potent power
The key to freedom
As you blossom and flower

The beauty you see
In the symbol of a dove
The unity of all
With the act of self-love

Don't give up
Don't give in
The magic is yours
Share the secret within

Heartbreak often elevates our fears. Unfortunately, we can't erase fears entirely, it's part of our DNA, but we can reduce them so that they have no power over us.

Have you found the magic sauce that helps dissolve your fears, dear one? Do you know it's inside of you and more potent than you know?

The magic sauce within all of us is love. When we give love, with all of our hearts, both to ourselves and others, we reduce our fears.

Love tells us we are enough, love tells us we belong, it tells us everything will be OK.

HEALING 18 – Write down five things you fear. Now look at that list and pour your magic sauce of love all over it. With the love sauce absorbed, write down what those five things look like now.

Did you see how your fears reduced? Did they become smaller when you allowed yourself to pour love over them? Did you see how much more clarity and calmness came through?

Love has such potency: it's something that you can only keep when you give it away. Imagine the magic sauce bottle re-filling the more you pour it out.

Give yourself and others the love you have and share the secret.

Daily reminder

- ♥ Three gratitudes
- ♥ Self-love into the mirror
- ♥ Meditation
- ♥ Laughter

Day 19

The universe guides
In the steps we take
The lessons we learn
And memories we make

Follow your heart
Let hope lead the way
With energy in abundance
As you take action today

Be resilient in your pursuits
Don't give up, you won't lose
Having trust in yourself
Is knowing it's love that you choose

Life is uncertain
It's challenging too
So give yourself the gift
Of just being you

There are many reasons to believe in what can't be seen. We can't see gravity, but we know its effect. We can't see oxygen, but we'd soon feel its absence.

The universe guiding our path isn't something that we can see; some of us may even choose to not believe, and that's OK; but it doesn't mean that there isn't a power greater than ourselves present amongst us.

We each have a role to play with the time we have and the lessons from our heartbreaks can spur us further forward if we allow ourselves to learn.

HEALING 19 – There are five words in the accompanying poem that make up the acronym HEART.

These are the principles to healing yourself. Find these five principles and access the wisdom from your own heart as to where you need to focus first. (Clue – The words are in the middle two verses and don't include the word heart).

We are always given a trail of breadcrumbs that lead us to where we are meant to be; we must first, however, make a decision to embark on the journey.

Daily reminder

- ♥ Three gratitudes
- ♥ Self-love into the mirror
- ♥ Meditation
- ♥ Laughter

Day 20

Are you committed
To travel the distance
Embrace your fears
Despite all the resistance

What could you achieve
Saying yes over no
Heeding your soul's voice
Where would you go

Commitment takes courage
Yes you do have to choose
To never give up
To be prepared to lose

To learn from mistakes
Adjusting your course as you go
Saying yes to the uncertainty
For you have new seeds to sow

To heal from heartbreak requires a commitment not to lose yourself in victim mode. This means not living in the past but focusing on the future you want to create. This means not staying stuck in the hurt but using it to propel you forward.

It means not saying 'I can't get through this' but changing it to 'I can get through this'. This means not making excuses when your life doesn't look as you want it to but taking responsibility to create the life you want.

We learn the hard way that we have complete choice over how we respond to events in our lives. Accepting that we have a choice means acknowledging our own role in moving ourselves forward.

HEALING 20 – Write a legacy statement. Think about who will remember you and how long they will remember you for. How do you want to be remembered by them and what do you want to be remembered for? Once you have written this down, take time to reflect on who you would need to be to fulfil this legacy statement.

When we remind ourselves of the impact we can have on the lives of others, it reminds us of the choice we have to transform any situation.

Choosing to give the best of us allows us to see the immense power we have to change the world around us simply by saying yes to what we can be.

Make your legacy meaningful to you, anything less is just another excuse to fail.

Daily reminder

- ♥ Three gratitudes
- ♥ Self-love into the mirror
- ♥ Meditation
- ♥ Laughter

Day 21

S low it down now
So you begin to see
The beauty of the journey
You embarked on to be free

You've come a long way
Travelled many a bumpy road
There are many more to travel
But it's time to lighten the load

Time to take a break
Time to take it slow
Acknowledge where you are
And look forward to where you'll go

Look back to connect the dots
And see the mystery unfold
The destination is revealing itself
Follow the rainbow to your gold

Slow down to acknowledge how far you have come on this journey. Healing isn't an overnight process and taking time to notice the progress you have made is imperative.

This journey can feel so isolating at times, but know you are not alone. Every human feels the pain of heartbreak in their lifetime and there is a collective knowing of this path that each of us travels in the becoming of ourselves.

The pain we experience is there to purify us so that we can emerge with greater humility, love and compassion for ourselves and others.

HEALING 21 – Today it's time to slow down and connect with nature. Acknowledge the season. Is it spring, summer, autumn or winter? Notice the changes that you see in the trees around you, notice the growth or the shedding of leaves. In what way are you in sync with the nature that surrounds you right now? Capture this moment with a photograph and acknowledge where you are and the peace you feel through slowing down.

The sadness will pass and you'll look back one day and see why slowing down to acknowledge where you are was so necessary to your growth.

Nature does not hurry; it knows that there is a time for everything. In times of deep pain, we wish it to be over quickly; trust the progress you have made already and trust the timing.

You are right on time.

Daily reminder

- ♥ Three gratitudes
- ♥ Self-love into the mirror
- ♥ Meditation
- ♥ Laughter

Day 22

F orgive yourself
  For when you fall short
Forgive yourself
The disempowering thought

Forgive yourself
For being misunderstood
Forgive yourself
For not doing what you should

Forgive yourself
The imperfections in you
Forgive yourself
For what you know to be true

Forgive yourself
That which you did not see
Forgive yourself
To set yourself free

In many cases heartbreak can leave us without closure: from the loss of a loved one, from the end of a relationship or perhaps from friendships dissolving.

When we don't get closure, dear one, we often have a million unanswered questions and it's hard not to keep revisiting the past trying to make sense of what has unfolded.

Many of us will start picking at our own imperfections and judging ourselves. Wishing perhaps that we'd done things or said things differently or had been able to see what was happening much more clearly.

It's easy to get caught in a cycle of self-blame and criticism. And get frustrated and hurt by the lack of understanding of why things turned out that way and wishing you could have the answers from others.

HEALING 22 – Write down all the feelings you have about yourself, the feelings you have for the person or people you are thinking about and the questions you have that remain unanswered.

Once you have all this written down commit to forgiving yourself for the self-judgement and to letting go of this burden of emotional baggage you carry. Light a candle, read the 'Forgive yourself' poem out loud and then burn the list you have written.

Life won't always give us the answers we crave and reliving the past and holding on to the hurt and pain does not serve us.

We can only influence the future to be better when we let go of wishing that we could change the past.

Daily reminder

- ♥ Three gratitudes
- ♥ Self-love into the mirror
- ♥ Meditation
- ♥ Laughter

Day 23

Goodbye old
Hello new
The moments passing
I acknowledge you

Lessons learned
Guide the way
To master oneself
Is what I seek today

To look within
Not without
To see the truth
Has no doubt

To take that step
Be not afraid
To shine the light
On the path that's laid

Passion my fuel
Purpose the driver
Love is the journey
My soul the survivor

Are you aware of the path that is laid ahead for you? What have you noticed about what you see?

Perhaps you haven't started looking ahead yet. Are you still looking backwards and finding it hard to let go?

Go easy on yourself and gently accept that the beauty of your light will shine if you let yourself be. It's time to master the wonder of who you are.

HEALING 23 – Write down three things you enjoy doing. Consider why you feel enjoyment from each one and to what extent this reveals to you what you are passionate about. It could be in a big or small way – don't overthink. Choose one of the things on your list to do today; one that might also bring enjoyment and help someone else too.

Passions are what bring us joy, but our purpose in life is how we use our passions to help others.

Choosing a purpose that is meaningful for us and that resonates in the way it helps others, will keep us committed to making time for that passion.

It's all too easy to drop the things we do just for ourselves, but when we see that what brings us joy can also help others, it's a powerful fuel that can drive us forward.

Daily reminder

- ♥ Three gratitudes
- ♥ Self-love into the mirror
- ♥ Meditation
- ♥ Laughter

Day 24

Smile beautiful
Let your eyes shine
I see power in your love
As you show me mine

Trust in your embrace
No doubt do I feel
The warmth of your love
In abundance you deal

Laughing as you play
Filling joy in my heart
These moments of wonder
Cherished in each day I start

Do you realise the power of your love and the impact it has in this world? At times of heartbreak it can be hard to see yourself and your love clearly.

The truth is that it's your own love for yourself that will ultimately heal you. When others see you flourish with the kindness and compassion you extend to yourself, you set an example for others to acknowledge their own love.

HEALING 24 – Write a list describing who you are and all the things you do that make you worthy of love. Make it a full list, don't hold back. Read this list out loud to yourself in front of a mirror. Notice how your body feels when you speak to yourself with kindness and compassion.

Does it feel awkward or uncomfortable? Well it shouldn't, dear one, because you are worthy of love. Re-read the list and absorb the loving energy into your body – allow yourself to feel the truth of who you are.

Smile and let your eyes shine, feel the words penetrate your skin and reach deep into your soul. You know these words are true but somewhere along the way you forgot.

It's time to rediscover the beauty and pure love that you are.

Daily reminder

- ♥ Three gratitudes
- ♥ Self-love into the mirror
- ♥ Meditation
- ♥ Laughter

Day 25

Believe in yourself
What might you see
The greatness within you
And all you could be

Nourish your mind
Body and spirit too
Listen for the call
To do what you do

You are a creator
With so much to give
Don't hold yourself back
You have a life to live

With joy in your heart
Leap forward to play
The adventure awaits
So don't delay

It's natural for us to want to hold on to memories of what we once had; it's not always easy to let go of what we lost or dreams that weren't fulfilled.

Trust that what you are going through will serve you in the future, allow yourself to see the gift your heartbreak offers. Desires will begin to get stronger and there are many ways still open for you to fulfil them.

Our heart is a muscle that has to strengthen after a break. Know that the pain you have experienced so far will lead you to break open in a way that you may have otherwise not have had access to. Don't see breaking open as something to be afraid of – there is beauty in this pain if you look. Much like a flower emerging from a tight bud or a butterfly from a cocoon.

HEALING 25 – Today is the time to channel your pain into creating something beautiful. It could be as simple as colouring in a book, drawing, writing a poem, writing a story, recording a podcast, making some music, singing a song, taking photographs or planting flowers.

Know that there is always beauty to be found in pain, some of the greatest books and art have been produced by those who have suffered greatly from heartbreak.

Give the world something wonderful to experience through your pain. Go forth – your creative adventure awaits you.

Daily reminder

- ♥ Three gratitudes
- ♥ Self-love into the mirror
- ♥ Meditation
- ♥ Laughter

Day 26

When you find yourself in darkness
Look up to see the light
When you feel that you are defeated
Trust in your courage to fight

When the wilderness calls you
Let your ego fall away
When you're far from home
Know your heart is where to stay

When all around you is chaos
Spread love wherever you go
When others are feeling lost
Share all that you already know

When you know you are always caught
Help others make the leap
When you recognise your purpose
Know it's your time to share, not keep

There is always contrast in life – where there is light there is dark. Where there is day there is night. Where there is happiness there is sadness. Where there is deep there is shallow. Where there is rising there is falling.

Recognising the contrasts in life helps us to know what we want for ourselves. When we experience the rough, we seek the smooth; the lows help us to appreciate the highs. Please don't reject or deny anything you experience, it's all there to bring you awareness of what you want.

Your greatest growth can come from your deepest pain. Allow contrast to be part of your life to help understand the wholeness of who you are.

HEALING 26 – Notice the contrasts that present themselves to you and how you feel in response to them. The contrasts that you experience help you discern what you want or don't want for yourself. Make a note of what is revealed about what you want – use what is presented to you during the day; the more you begin to pay attention, the more awareness you gain about yourself.

Don't resist any pain you may feel, accept it and acknowledge it as a guide to discovering more about what you want.

Understand that you have the ability to bring calm to the chaos and that you can only find yourself by getting lost.

Trust in the power of contrast working for you and not against you.

Daily reminder

- ♥ Three gratitudes
- ♥ Self-love into the mirror
- ♥ Meditation
- ♥ Laughter

Day 27

Do you see me
Like I see me

My eyes sparkle
And my smile is bright
With my heart wide open
I bathe in the light

I have been broken
My wounds still heal
Whilst fear threatens to consume me
It's love that I feel

I see myself clearly
I love all that I see
I'm yours for the taking
Just being me

Seeing yourself clearly, dear one, is the greatest gift you can give this world. When you see yourself clearly, you'll see that there is only love.

We can get caught up in a narrative that says we aren't good enough or that we aren't loveable as we are. This is just a story and one that keeps us from seeing the truth of who we are and the magnificence we can be.

When we break, it allows light to enter and enables us to shine from within. We have much to give and seeing our love radiate out from our deepest part through the pain we have experienced is necessary for us to fulfil our true potential.

HEALING 27 – Today is a day to appreciate light, to bathe in sunlight and allow it to penetrate your skin. Go to a beach or a park and enjoy the sunshine, close your eyes and feel the warmth of its rays hold you and nourish you. If it's not a sunny day, choose a quiet warm place and visualise somewhere you love that is normally bathed in sunshine. Feel the light radiate within you and know that you will shine brightly and smile again.

Don't let the light within you be extinguished by your pain, let yourself be nourished by the sun and know that each day it pours more and more light into your soul so that you can shine again and let the world know of the love that you embody.

Daily reminder

- ♥ Three gratitudes
- ♥ Self-love into the mirror
- ♥ Meditation
- ♥ Laughter

Day 28

Oh, how I wish
That you could see
Accepting yourself
Would set you free

The shackles that bind
Are just perceptions of you
You're holding on tight
To what is not true

Fear of your greatness
Is too much to bear
So you hold yourself back
Into the abyss you stare

But who are you serving
When you hide away
Your greatness is for sharing
So step forward today

Own who you are
For all to see
Show them the way
And set them free

Heartbreak often leaves us questioning whether we are worthy of love. It can cause us to retreat rather than step forward into the fullest expression of who we are.

Showing ourselves to the world in all our glory requires us to own and accept who we are. We often fear what others think, we fear being rejected and looking foolish.

But when we begin to accept and love ourselves exactly as we are it frees us from these restrictions and allows us to step into a new world of possibilities. This doesn't mean that we don't seek to constantly improve ourselves, it means that when we do, it's from a place of love, not fear.

HEALING 28 – Today's healing is about being inspired by others and learning how they stepped into the fullest expression of themselves and took a journey of self-discovery through their pain. Take some time to find and read an inspiring book or article by someone you admire deeply. Learn more about how they successfully navigated adversity, and the pain they experienced to reach acceptance and love for themselves.

Books can be like windows to the souls of their writers: often there is great wisdom in the lessons they have learned.

Remembering that pain is universal and taking time to read others' stories will help you recognise that this pain, if you allow it, can break you open to the fullest and most beautiful expression of yourself.

Daily reminder

- ♥ Three gratitudes
- ♥ Self-love into the mirror
- ♥ Meditation
- ♥ Laughter

Day 29

I opened my heart
And set myself free
Declaring my love
For no other than thee

Whilst careful with my words
I left nothing unsaid
But you didn't feel the same
And so my heart bled

Where once I'd be broken
As the tears threaten to fall
Today I feel lighter
Knowing I gave my all

You see I'm not afraid
Of loving you and all of me
I'm enriched for this feeling
Of vulnerability

Let truth be thy goal
And let love lead the way
Broken hearts will heal
With the dawn of a new day

Inner peace is what I found
By opening up my heart
I pulled down the wall around me
For my happiness, my fresh start

Baring your heart and soul is the most vulnerable thing you can do; it is also the most courageous.

Opening up your heart and expressing what you feel can be incredibly daunting, especially when it can lead to rejection from another. But a life of regret often comes from not having had the courage to say the things we wanted to say or do the things we wanted to do.

We only have this one precious life; we can miss the beauty of it if we don't allow ourselves to find peace in the expression of our truth.

The more we suppress our truth and avoid expressing what needs to be expressed, the more it seeks to surface and the harder it is to heal and move forward.

HEALING 29 – Today is your opportunity to release your current thoughts and feelings onto paper. Allow yourself to unburden fully, don't hold anything back – write them all down until you have nothing further that needs to be said.

Read your words back out loud and see what you feel. Let go of all the emotions that you have been holding in and observe what arises.

Purging our thoughts on paper and speaking them out loud can take the power out of the pain we feel. We begin to see life as it is; by releasing any inner tension we begin to experience peace.

Give yourself the gift of peace today.

Daily reminder

- ♥ Three gratitudes
- ♥ Self-love into the mirror
- ♥ Meditation
- ♥ Laughter

Day 30

I observe with wonder
At the synchronicity I see
When the pieces of the puzzle
Join together for me

The magic that is unlocked
Is so hard to describe
But the evidence is shown
With the love of my tribe

Following my truth
Has led me here
To discover myself
I had nothing to fear

My joy in being
Is overflowing in me
Like a waterfall of love
Flowing into the sea

Everything happens for a reason; even the pain we are given to endure teaches us more about ourselves.

It's difficult, if not impossible, to connect the dots looking forward, but we can connect them looking back. We begin to see how all the things that have happened in our lives – big and little, good and bad – have allowed us to become the person we are.

HEALING 30 – Draw a horizontal timeline on a piece of paper marking your age from birth to now. Then, in a different colour, draw a second line, similar to a wavy heart-rate line depicting the highs and lows of your life journey to date, overlaid on your life timeline.

Mark each event that represented a high or low in your life timeline and note what your experiences reveal about the person you are now. What are you now able to do as a result of these experiences?

Seeing how your life is made up of highs and lows will help you discover the growth that came with each event. What you may begin to notice is that your biggest growth comes from the deepest lows. Pain often acts as a catalyst for change.

Trust that this journey is leading you to where you need to be, to meet the people you need to meet, to learn the lessons that you need to learn in order to make the difference that only you are uniquely placed to make.

Follow the truth of your journey so far; acknowledge that this moment and pain will pass and continue to lead you to fulfil your soul's purpose.

Daily reminder

- ♥ Three gratitudes
- ♥ Self-love into the mirror
- ♥ Meditation
- ♥ Laughter

Day 31

Until we shall meet
My heart beats without fear
Trusting you'll find me
I wait for you my dear

Life without hope
Seems fruitless to me
Like a day without breathing
How can we be

I use this time wisely
Uncovering the magic of each day
Fulfilled with every moment
As you make your way

I'll sense when you are here
As my heart skips a beat
The smile on your face
As I say I love you my sweet

It's time to discover yourself and reveal your magic, dear one. There is lots to do and little time, all the dreams you have to manifest and the wonder in your life to be created. Don't hide in sadness, it's time for action.

You need to be the catalyst and accept that everything in your life is working for you, not against you – even if you don't believe this right now, have trust that it is true.

HEALING 31 – Today is the day to discover your magic. Write a list of all the things that put a smile on your face. Write down all the things that make you sad. Now every time you find yourself feeling sad swap it for something that puts a smile on your face. When you see how easy it is to make yourself feel good, you'll see how quickly you can manifest the life you want.

When you realise that you have the power to change your emotional state by making a choice that works for you rather than against you, everything changes.

This isn't to minimise your pain, but it lets you acknowledge an inner strength that only comes to life when you allow yourself to access it.

You have the capacity to change how you view life around you by altering your outlook. When you choose to activate what you want to feel rather than accept how you actually feel, you start to find ways to make that a reality.

Changing to a more positive emotional state fuels your energy and will create abundance in your life.

Daily reminder

- ♥ Three gratitudes
- ♥ Self-love into the mirror
- ♥ Meditation
- ♥ Laughter

Day 32

Thank you for your vulnerability
For letting me see you
Thank you for dropping the façade
And for being true

Life has its challenges
We often face them alone
But letting others in
You find kindness you've never known

We all seek connection
To love and to belong
Sharing who you are
As beautiful as birdsong

You don't have to be tough
Our fears are all the same
Open the doors to your heart
And let love be the aim

A problem shared is a problem halved is a saying that many of us have heard, but many of us fear sharing the truth about what we feel.

What is clear, however, this journey called life isn't meant to be travelled alone. There are people who love you if you let yourself see them, dear one, and allow them the greatest privilege we all have – the opportunity to help another human through kindness.

HEALING 32 – Today it's time to gather the people you love around you, whether it's for a night in with your favourite food and party games, a night out hitting the dance floor, or maybe a beautiful day out enjoying a lovely lunch.

Don't deny yourself the opportunity to be loved and cared for by others when you feel down. Choose people who never judge you or expect you to always be happy; ones who accept you just as you are and are willing to be there for you no matter what.

Being around those who love us allows us to recognise that we all need connection and it helps us to heal considerably faster than doing it alone, especially if it includes a wonderful warm hug.

Daily reminder
- ♥ Three gratitudes
- ♥ Self-love into the mirror
- ♥ Meditation
- ♥ Laughter

Day 33

Take a step forward
  Please don't be afraid
I'll meet you halfway
In love we will trade

I'm willing to give
As much as you need
To help you through
The darkness you feed

No judgement here
Just love from my heart
Will you let me in
So we are not apart

Let go of your shame
And clear your view
Your hurt is not serving
The greatness of you

You have so much to give
And your heart is pure
Filled with love
Right through to your core

Many people believe that heartbreak leaves them shattered and broken into thousands of pieces. The truth is that, if you allow it, heartbreak can break you open to reveal more of who you are.

Breaking open allows you to access a part of you that you may never have otherwise discovered. Through heartbreak you can find out what you truly care about and see if there are any areas in yourself that require healing.

When we hold onto our hurt we don't allow ourselves the growth that comes from breaking open.

HEALING 33 – Notice what wisdom your heartbreak has revealed to you about who you are. Let go of any shame you have carried and clear your view. How has this heartbreak helped you see what you didn't see before? What can you now do with that knowledge to grow into the person you want to be? Take the answers you have from this healing and write down a new life manifesto that honours the person you are now and the desires you have for yourself and the world around you.

We each carry so much wisdom inside us but we often fail to look there to find the answers. You were broken open for a reason and your growth will serve a much greater purpose when you let in the light and no longer feed your darkness.

Daily reminder

- ♥ Three gratitudes
- ♥ Self-love into the mirror
- ♥ Meditation
- ♥ Laughter

Day 34

Today I smile
With a deep knowing
That my future is now
As I keep growing

The smallest of steps
Can take you far
Progress is the key
To unlocking your star

In the face of uncertainty
Let courage be your guide
Choosing freedom over fear
You get to decide

Observe your journey
As you unleash your power
No holding back
Now is the hour

Now is the time to change your future. It all starts with a decision to choose the life you want.

It can be overwhelming to think about where you want to be and sometimes it can feel like you will never get there.

However, when you commit to moving forward and not giving up, even when you don't know how to get there, you will notice that the path begins to reveal itself.

Perhaps you want to write a book, maybe you want to learn to dance or study something new – it doesn't matter what it is – the moment to make a choice for your future self is now.

HEALING 34 – You know the life you want. Don't let it slip through your fingers. In Healing 16 you identified what you wanted to be celebrating this time next year. Revisit what you wrote – does it still resonate deeply for you? Is it really what you want? If yes, what next step can you take today to continue the momentum and bring it to life?

If you find yourself resisting or procrastinating, recognise that this means you are not in alignment with what you say you want. When you are truly aligned, action will follow: nothing will hold you back from going after your goal.

Even the smallest step will get you closer to the life you desire; the worst thing you can do is stand still and watch the world around you move forward and leave you behind.

Step by step, little by little – don't stop now, dear one, you've come so far.

Daily reminder

- ♥ Three gratitudes
- ♥ Self-love into the mirror
- ♥ Meditation
- ♥ Laughter

Day 35

You are the love
That set me free
Broke my heart
To let me be

I once was lost
But now I'm found
Feeling blessed
I kiss the ground

The sun shines bright
The sky is clear
The journey alone
I no longer fear

Abundance of love
I'm guaranteed
It lies within me
All I need

It's not until we are lost that we begin to seek to find ourselves. Heartbreak brings with it many blessings that we otherwise would never have had access to.

Heartbreak can break us free from the assumption of a life we thought we should have had. It's scary and can be hard to face up to, but the truth is that it brings an opportunity to know ourselves in ways we might never have otherwise explored.

This is precious time, don't be scared; you won't be journeying alone for long. There are people that you are meant to meet, and you have gifts that you are meant to share.

When you begin to find yourself, you learn to see yourself differently and see parts of you that were previously hidden. It's time to ground yourself so that you are ready to embrace this next chapter in your life.

HEALING 35 – Choose a spot in nature that always makes you feel at home. Take your shoes off and feel the earth beneath your feet. Close your eyes and feel the energy of Mother Nature grounding you. Take a photo to record this spot in your journal.

Whenever you feel lost, anchor yourself to this moment. With Mother Nature you are safe, and you are held: you are exactly where you are meant to be. Trust your journey.

Daily reminder

- ♥ Three gratitudes
- ♥ Self-love into the mirror
- ♥ Meditation
- ♥ Laughter

Day 36

I surrender
To set myself free
From my own expectations
Of how life should be

To trust what is meant
Will find a way
As I focus my efforts
On living each day

My dreams for my future
I continue to see
The grip now loosened
To allow them to be

Surrender is not easy
I stumble and fall
But the universe reminds me
It takes care of it all

I need not worry
About the path ahead
One step at a time
To my destination I'm led

Loosening the grip when you feel out of control is the last thing you will want to do, but it is the most necessary if you want to heal. Surrender isn't always easy, but it is needed to enable you to flow towards what you are meant for.

It's time to stop swimming against the flow of the river, it's tiring; as hard as you try, you'll come to realise it's not the direction for you. It's time to flip onto your back and allow yourself to be carried by the water and go with the flow.

HEALING 36 – Today is time for play and to surrender to the feeling of joy. Choose something fun to do and trust that when you allow yourself to flow with life that you'll be carried to where you want to be. You don't have to put in any effort, allow your enthusiasm to guide you.

What you begin to discover with play is that it relaxes your thinking mind and helps you access the true intentions for your life; things that really matter will surface and you can let go of the things that don't serve you.

When you follow your feelings of joy, you align with your truest intentions and you'll begin to see how surrender is beginning to serve your highest self: joy will reveal your direction.

Daily reminder

- ♥ Three gratitudes
- ♥ Self-love into the mirror
- ♥ Meditation
- ♥ Laughter

Day 37

The pictures we paint
Of our lives for the world
How accurate is the image
In the reflection we've swirled

The smiles and the laughter
Our dances and our song
The story we have captured
Is it where we belong

We radiate the light
And bury deep the dark
Real stories remain untold
But they leave their mark

The more you run
The faster they chase
Willing you to acknowledge
Your truth with grace

Paint your picture
Paint it true
Embrace all of your story
Be free being you

What picture are you painting of your life for the world to see? Does it reflect who you truly are and the person you wish to be?

Great freedom comes with being all of you, owning both your light and your dark too. No human has only light in their life, each one suffers hurt and pain at some point in their journey.

Our heartbreak sometimes comes because we haven't allowed ourselves to accept all of who we are. We continue to run from the truth of ourselves as we paint pictures of the perfect life for others to accept us.

HEALING 37 – Today it's time to ask yourself if there is anything you are holding back in being your true self. Are there truths about you that need to be shared with the people that matter to you? It's time to paint your picture and paint it true. Don't let untold stories leave their mark on you, the scars only get deeper with time.

Healing isn't just about bubble baths and candles, in order to truly step into the future you want, it's necessary to complete on the past.

Don't bury anything that needs to be addressed – it will only resurface even when you think it won't, the universe always finds a way to teach us the lessons we most need to learn.

Acknowledge your truth with grace and be free being yourself.

Daily reminder

♥ Three gratitudes
♥ Self-love into the mirror

♥ Meditation
♥ Laughter

Day 38

Oh Mirror Mirror
On the wall
The image you reflect
Does it match at all

Is the person I craft
For the world and me
Truly aligned
To who I want to be

Is what I do
And who I see
Reflecting back
The image I agree

I look closer
Take it all in
Choose my truth
Let my life begin

When you look in the mirror what are you seeing? Do you see your laughter lines and recall all the moments that made you smile?

Do you see the sparkle in your eyes, the light that's captured the magic of the world around you? Do you see the warmth of your smile brightening someone else's day?

What image is your mirror reflecting back to you? Do you see the beauty of what is being reflected?

It's easy to look in the mirror and only see the flaws, but what we focus on we magnify. Isn't it time to magnify the image you want to be reflected back to you?

HEALING 38 – Today it's time to look at photos of the people in the world that have inspired you. What do you see when you look at them? What do you notice about the qualities and energy they exude that don't relate to their physical beauty?

We can spend our time looking in the mirror wishing we looked different or we can choose to mirror the qualities that we most admire in others.

The most attractive people recognise that beauty is more than skin deep and that you can have timeless beauty that doesn't fade when you focus on sharing the beauty that's within you with the world around you.

Align yourself to the beauty within you and those around you can't but help falling in love with you.

Daily reminder

- ♥ Three gratitudes
- ♥ Self-love into the mirror
- ♥ Meditation
- ♥ Laughter

Day 39

Know who you are
Transcend the status quo
Mobilise the masses
Wherever you go

Move with purpose
As you share your story
Be humble with your message
Don't trade your passion for glory

Your message is your gift
Through your hardship you earned
To make others' lives easy
With the lessons you learned

The time is now
Shine your light
Stop playing small
Let your fire burn bright

Heartache brings with it a huge gift through the lessons that we learn in the struggle to overcome the grief and sadness that often accompanies it.

The greatest stories, songs, films and books have often come from the deep source of pain people have felt during heartbreak. Heartbreak is necessary to evolve into the fullest expression of who we are.

It breaks us open and reveals the magic within each and every one of us.

How many people do you know who have never experienced any kind of heartbreak at all? It would be impossible to live a full life and never experience it.

What does that tell us? It tells us that heartbreak is a necessary path to personal growth. The gifts you have to give to the world can, and most likely will, come from your most difficult experiences.

HEALING 39 – Today can you share what your heartbreak has unlocked in you that previously you didn't recognise in yourself? What has it shown that you are passionate about now? What would now be a gift to others as result of your experience?

Simply sharing what you learn here is a gift.

This book wouldn't be in your hands if it weren't for heartbreak. Look for the gold: don't dwell on what has been lost but what you have gained.

There is much you can see when you allow yourself to look.

Daily reminder

- ♥ Three gratitudes
- ♥ Self-love into the mirror
- ♥ Meditation
- ♥ Laughter

Day 40

Walk your own path
Find your own way
Be open to adventure
At the dawn of each new day

Journey into the wilderness
You will have to brave it alone
Take one step at a time
To your destination you will be shown

A destination where there are others
That have braved the wilderness too
Where you no longer seek to belong
Because you do by just being you

Smile as you arrive
You'll know when you are there
You'll be standing alone
But in togetherness you will share

No need to be afraid
Though the journey may be long
You'll be guided by your truth
To the light to sing your song

It can feel scary walking our own path, especially when we have a strong desire to share the journey with another, but for one reason or another have to walk this path alone.

The wilderness that calls you is inviting you to explore who you are at your very core. This journey is one that each and every human has to take during their lifetime – it's a rite of passage and a requirement to understand yourself better and to see yourself more clearly.

Others have taken this journey too; they will be familiar with the route even though your paths will differ. The pain of heartbreak is a calling for you to go deep in discovering what you are on the inside.

To find the pure love inside you that flows through you and to you, you have to allow yourself to be open to it.

HEALING 40 – It's time for another adventure by going into the wilderness. It's time to mark a weekend in your calendar when you will take another trip to find out more about yourself.

Whether it's a retreat with others on the same journey, or a solo trip trekking and camping – your heart knows what you need even if it scares you a little. Trust and go, allow yourself to know.

The wilderness is a place where we are all called, to embrace the truth of who we are. The pain you feel is urging you to find your peace within, allow it to happen.

Daily reminder

- ♥ Three gratitudes
- ♥ Self-love into the mirror
- ♥ Meditation
- ♥ Laughter

Day 41

I choose growth
So I embrace the pain
I choose rainbows
So I embrace the rain

I choose freedom
So I embrace the wilderness
I choose fulfilment
So I embrace the emptiness

I choose love
So I embrace vulnerability
I choose my heart
So I embrace my fragility

I choose me
So I embrace being alone
I choose trust
So I embrace the unknown

I choose you
So I embrace letting go
I choose yes
So I embrace hearing no

Life is full of contrasts as we mentioned previously. Many of us will understand that to know the light we must experience the dark.

To have growth there is a level of pain we must experience. The contrasts in life help us tune into what we want through understanding what we don't want.

When you are in heartbreak you endure immense sadness; it seems impossible to imagine life ever feeling as good as it once did. But as with the seasons that come and go, the rainbows that come with the sunshine after the rain, we must trust that our pain and sadness will pass and lead us forward into another chapter of joy.

HEALING 41 – Observe the poem for guidance and write a list of five things you wish for yourself in your life. Then write down their corresponding contrasts that you would be willing to embrace for you to experience these five chosen things.

When you accept that contrasts are there to show you the way to the path you have chosen, your resistance to them decreases and you open yourself up to welcoming more of what you want.

Daily reminder

- ♥ Three gratitudes
- ♥ Self-love into the mirror
- ♥ Meditation
- ♥ Laughter

Day 42

You are needed
There is a part for you to play
The future may not be clear
But there is a reason for you to stay

The journey may be hard
Perhaps you feel all alone
But know that you are loved
And the answer will be shown

Trust in the path
Follow to where the breadcrumbs lead
You have a purpose to live
So do not let your heart bleed

Your intuition already knows
The role you have to play
Whilst it may appear scary
Unleash the courage within you to stay

What if the path for you to follow has already been laid? What if the intention for your life is to simply follow the path guided by the breadcrumbs left for you?

It seems difficult to believe, but how might life unfold if you follow the path of least resistance? If least resistance were about choosing thoughts that feel good and then following where they lead you – where would you be?

Your body intuitively knows when you are out of alignment, usually you know this too when you don't feel good in yourself. This is your body's way of guiding you to choose more helpful thoughts. When you feel better, you do better.

HEALING 42 – **Acknowledge that there is a reason for you being here, even though you may not see it right now. Notice what you feel, this will connect you to your inner guidance system. Each time you notice a thought that doesn't feel good, change it to one that does.**

Keep up this practice to strengthen your alignment and jot down what you notice happening. When you start feeling good, the energy around you acts like a magnet, drawing things to you that match the energy you emit.

Allow yourself to discover what you can attract with this simple shift of focus.

Daily reminder

♥ Three gratitudes
♥ Self-love into the mirror
♥ Meditation

♥ Laughter
♥ Connect to your inner guidance system

Day 43

The bliss I feel
I cannot describe
The joy in my heart
In finding my tribe

The brave and wild
The movers and shakers
The unapologetic
The music makers

Freeing myself
The shackles unbound
A place of love
No judgement found

I travelled a journey
But did not go far
The tribe was within me
Shining light like a star

Heartbreak allows us to examine our lives in a way we may not otherwise have explored. It brings an opportunity to reset and recalibrate the environment around us. The people we have in our lives influence the energy we experience, so it's important to be aware if the energy is helping or hindering you.

When you consider the people around you, who have you surrounded yourself with? How do you feel when you are with them? Are they supportive? Kind? Compassionate? Do their actions show you how they feel about you?

The tribe you surround yourself with will influence your life experience. For better or worse they have a bearing on how comfortable you feel in being yourself. You've already completed a relationship audit in Healing 14 – this takes it a little further.

HEALING 43 – Revisit the list of people you noted previously and add others to the list if there are new people in your life who you regularly interact with. This time identify the people that bring out the best in you and those that bring out the worst in you. If you are authentically yourself with people who only ever bring out the worst in you, then you need to make some tough choices. Make a decision to choose a tribe that you can not only be yourself with but that wants to see you succeed and helps you grow and stretch yourself. Now is the right time to let go of people who don't serve you being your best self.

It's never easy to let go of people, but to have more of what you want you have to create space by removing what you don't want. Allow yourself to be who you were born to be, and only keep close those people who will never knowingly dim your light.

Daily reminder

- ♥ Three gratitudes
- ♥ Self-love into the mirror
- ♥ Meditation
- ♥ Laughter
- ♥ Connect to your inner guidance system

Day 44

Faith what does it mean
Believing in something before it is seen

I used to fear but now I see
I must trust in my journey to just be me

Action is necessary I know I must do
To not act is to deny that which is true

We each have gifts to be discovered and shared
Along with our stories our hearts to be bared

Time is our friend the now we must embrace
Cherish the moments as we run our own race

Smile and laugh, joy is what heals
Time to bathe in the love our heart feels

We often feel the fear that accompanies heartbreak and it's easy for us to wonder if we will ever feel joy and be whole again.

We lose ourselves by seeking certainty in our lives and forget what it means to have trust that life is working for us. It's easy to compare ourselves to others and feel the discomfort that the comparison brings.

When we compare ourselves, we move out of alignment with our own true path. We lose connection with what is available to us by refusing to accept where we are now relative to where others are.

What kind of future would you create for yourself if you truly believed you will be in a better place than where you are today? What would you wish for yourself if you trusted that everything that has happened has led you closer to a reality that brings out the fullest expression of yourself in this world?

HEALING 44 – Today it's time to acknowledge that you are running your own race. What gifts do you see in yourself that will bring joy and laughter to your world and the world of those around you? What action can you take today that shows off the gifts you bring?

Your gift can be the smallest of gestures that could make the biggest difference in someone's life if you allow yourself to share it.

Make peace with yourself and stay in your own lane.

Daily reminder

- ♥ Three gratitudes
- ♥ Self-love into the mirror
- ♥ Meditation
- ♥ Laughter
- ♥ Connect to your inner guidance system

Day 45

When it gets hard
What do you choose
Do you run away
Or fight not to lose

This too shall pass
I've heard it said
So live when you're living
We'll soon be dead

The path less travelled
Is not for all
Perhaps just for those
That are willing to fall

This one precious life
With much to learn
Myself realisation
Is what I seek to earn

Are you still thinking about your heartbreak? At times heartbreak can feel all-consuming; it's natural to want the pain and the hurt to disappear.

Sometimes it can feel like life would be so much easier if we didn't love so hard. That if we didn't give so much of ourselves then the pain of loss wouldn't be so bad.

It's a choice we all have available to us – to limit the love we allow ourselves to give and therefore allow ourselves to receive. But that's not the answer.

The contrasts we feel with the pain help us to become clearer about what we really want. The contrasts that we experience in life guide us daily to understand what is in alignment with our desires.

HEALING 45 – Notice if you have refrained from giving yourself fully to something for fear of rejection, hurt or failure. What have you stopped yourself from feeling and doing? What do you believe you are missing out on as a result?

Many of us forget to live when we are living, always looking for ways to avoid pain and numbing our experience of life in its truest richness. We focus on the destination and forget that life is only ever a series of moments on this journey.

A happy life is not simply made up of happy moments. There have to be sad moments too, but there is bliss in accepting that everything in life is working for you, not against you.

Free yourself from the fear by continuing to choose love – it's the only way to live a full life.

Daily reminder

- ♥ Three gratitudes
- ♥ Self-love into the mirror
- ♥ Meditation
- ♥ Laughter
- ♥ Connect to your inner guidance system

Day 46

Something's missing
You feel it inside
What is it
You cannot decide

You know there is a gap
A space to fill
You won't understand it
Until you fall still

Listen intently
To your soul within
For it has the clarity
On where to begin

The answers are known
It's just that you don't see
For them to be revealed
You just have to be

We can spend a lifetime searching for something that has been within us all along. When we pay attention, we see that our emotions give us access to discovering whether we are in alignment with who we are and what we want.

The question is whether you are paying attention to what your emotions are telling you.

Often, we sense a gap between the lives we are living and what we really want. We struggle to identify exactly what it is and how to get there. When you become still you slow the negative thoughts that cloud your view.

Slowing these thoughts reduces their hold and gives you the opportunity to move towards what you do want with much more ease. It's like choosing to flow with the current of the river rather than trying to swim upstream against it.

HEALING 46 – Today's practice is about mindfulness and reconnecting to your inner guidance system. Take ten deep and slow breaths in and out. Count to five as you breathe in and count to five as you breathe out. Feel yourself breathing in positive emotions and breathing out negative emotions.

As you connect with your body, slowing down the active thoughts in your mind, you allow yourself to open up and create lightness and peace within you.

You recognise that acting from a place of negative emotion doesn't lead to what you desire. This breathing exercise moves you to a more positive place that brings greater clarity on your next step.

This place of positive emotion increases the likelihood of you manifesting what you want.

Daily reminder

- ♥ Three gratitudes
- ♥ Self-love into the mirror
- ♥ Meditation
- ♥ Laughter
- ♥ Connect to your inner guidance system

Day 47

I am a phenomenal woman
Said Maya Angelou
Do you see this in yourself
And know it to be true

Take off your blindfold
It is time to see
The power of your heart
As you are meant to be

Your inner mastery
Lets your magic shine
Don't be shy now
This is your time

Step forth brave one
And take a bow
You as you are
Are sure to wow

What would you notice about yourself if you acknowledged how phenomenal you are? What qualities would you see?

We usually find it easier to see what we like about other people rather than identify what we like about ourselves. When we start to see ourselves more clearly and see the goodness that we have within, we open ourselves to a new brighter reality. However, it is only accessible to us when we pay attention to our own truth.

Recognising the good in others is only possible because of the goodness in ourselves – you can't recognise something that you don't already have yourself.

HEALING 47 – Imagine yourself taking a bow in front of an audience. What did you share of yourself? What are they applauding you for? If you weren't shy, what would you allow others to see? Close your eyes and let the images come to you. No effort is required, just relax, enjoy and explore what comes up.

Sharing what's within you is your unique gift to give. Often, we don't even know what that gift is until we've been broken open through heartbreak.

Opening up and letting the light shine within, allows us to access the hidden depth of our being and to know the wonder of who we are.

When we see our phenomenal selves, we feel alive – trust in that knowing, it's there to guide you.

Daily reminder

- ♥ Three gratitudes
- ♥ Self-love into the mirror
- ♥ Meditation
- ♥ Laughter
- ♥ Connect to your inner guidance system

Day 48

I feel the shift
Somewhere deep inside
A conscious awareness
I need not hide

Stepping into my power
I feel my body shake
The pulsing vibration
As I begin to awake

The truth within
I see it clearly now
Lights beckon
The way of the Tao

The infinite embrace
Of a love so true
Nurturing and kind
Do you feel it too?

I was once lost
But now I'm found
The peace inside
Growing unbound

Can you imagine a love that is so nurturing, so tender, so fulfilling and true? Can you imagine a love that is infinite, enduring and abundant in its giving to you?

A love that understands exactly what you need and what you deserve. A love that doesn't need you to ask, because it knows you better than you know yourself.

Your ability to imagine this love exists because this love is present within you and for you; it is accessible when you allow yourself to receive it. Imagine a love like that for yourself from yourself.

HEALING 48 – This all-powerful love is yours for the taking. It will fill your heart with pure joy as you feel it unfold in the fullness of who you are. Ask yourself who you would become and what might you achieve in the world if you loved yourself like that.

Take a note of what arises and recognise the power of your inner being's love for you to achieve your highest self, and the potential it unlocks in you to transform the world around you.

You can never feel lost when you appreciate yourself at this level. The unconditional presence of your inner being's love for you is limitless and will leave you free to create the riches you desire.

Embrace this, dear one. It is your truth calling you, let go of your resistance and allow your love and awareness to grow.

Daily reminder

- ♥ Three gratitudes
- ♥ Self-love into the mirror
- ♥ Meditation
- ♥ Laughter
- ♥ Connect to your inner guidance system

Day 49

Go forth dearest one
Don't hide in fear
You have much to give
This much is clear

Your path will weave
And wind a way
Your mission is to follow
Where it leads each day

You may not know
And that's OK
Take that step forward
Because life's a play

It's not what you know
But what you think
That manifests your hope
Or causes you to sink

The power of thought
You must harness today
It's your path to serenity
So don't delay

The life we experience is very much dependent on our thoughts, dear one, and choosing our thoughts is a primary factor in changing our reality.

Harnessing positive thoughts when our feelings are not aligned is incredibly challenging; in order to change our reality we must change how we feel.

Positive thinking requires positive feeling.

HEALING 49 – Today it's time to reconnect to your feelings of joy. Moments of magic where you have a sparkle in your eyes and a warm smile on your face. It's time to choose that feeling. Look around you, what can you see that brings you joy? What can you touch that shows you that you still have an abundance of happiness within? What can you hear or see that makes you laugh?

As you begin to feel deeply again, your emotions remind you that all is not lost; despite the tears, you can still find joy and laughter. You'll notice your thoughts will shift from a place of hopelessness to a place of hope, from doubt to belief and from not knowing to knowing that everything is always working out for you.

The more you focus on choosing to feel good, the more you change the reality you experience. It's OK to start small, just keep watching what happens the more you practise.

Daily reminder

- ♥ Three gratitudes
- ♥ Self-love into the mirror
- ♥ Meditation
- ♥ Laughter
- ♥ Connect to your inner guidance system

Day 50

L ove me tender
Love me true
Here I am
In love with you

I resisted at first
I couldn't see
The beauty within
Calling out to me

I finally realised
You had it all
Everything I needed
I just had to fall

I surrendered the search
I found my match
The mirror reflecting
My beautiful catch

I smiled knowing
I needed no more
I'd finally found
What I'd been searching for

We have always had everything we needed within us if only we allow ourselves to see. We let our fears hide the beauty that radiates from within us if only we allow ourselves to shine.

Sometimes we have to fall, dear one, to break our hearts open for the light to shine through.

The healing journey can feel like a slow death at times, but the reality is that just like a caterpillar's journey to becoming a butterfly, we too have to relinquish our old forms to embrace our ability to fly.

Today you will see that you are ready to fly.

HEALING 50 – Take a look in the mirror. Are you seeing yourself clearly? Can you see the love that you've always been looking for staring right back at you? Can you see the sparkle in your eyes and the warmth of your smile? Give yourself a loving hug with a deep knowing that you are beautiful. You are more than enough just as you are, dear one.

What you are searching for is right here with you; don't forget to love yourself because in doing so you show others how to love you too.

Self-love, as you have learned, is a daily practice, and now you are on this path, continue to practise kindness and compassion for who you are. You are always worthy of love and you have so much to give.

You've come a very long way, dear one, and travelled a difficult road; but your heart is much stronger than before. Your pain will come, and it will go; but the love you have for yourself will endure.

Calmness exudes from your inner being and you have a deep knowing that all you desire is available to you. To your beautiful new heart song, let's raise a glass.

The path forward

If you kept your commitment to yourself and completed the fifty days of healings you will know and feel the deepest connection to yourself.

The journey you have taken has unwrapped the gift of who you are and the contribution you make to the world.

Your healing was the path for you to find yourself, taking you from darkness into the light. Each day that you took a step forward, you have shown that you have the courage and resilience to stay the course and not give up. Your journal is your keepsake, a map that you created to find your treasure – the true unconditional love within you. A map that will always lead you home to yourself.

The work you have done towards your healing has been deeply reflective and much more will continue to reveal itself over the coming weeks and months. Allow yourself to receive what comes to you.

You've set powerful intentions for yourself and now you have an increased level of awareness about yourself and the world around you; this will help you move forward with renewed energy and clarity.

Don't underestimate yourself or ever question your worth – the love that you are is what is needed in this world.

Trust that those who are worthy of receiving your love will understand and truly know what a treasure they have in you.

Go forth, dear one, and please continue to light up the world with your heart.

Acknowledgements

Thank you to my lost loves for leading my heart to break open and strengthen in its healing to find a love like no other.

Thank you to my beautiful family and friends who continue to support and inspire me to grow and live a heart-aligned life.

Thank you to my dear friend Gail Murdoch for the gentle loving nudge to get this book published and share the love I discovered, with you.

The Author

Glin's own journey of healing after heartbreak led her to find deeper meaning and purpose to her life. In healing and following her heart, she moved from a small village in South Buckinghamshire, England, to start a new life in Sydney, Australia. Leaving a successful corporate career in finance, she started her own business, Heart of Human. Now, as an executive coach and leadership consultant, Glin works with women who seek to reveal the power of their own hearts to feel unstoppable in creating and living a life they love.

🌐 www.heartofhuman.com

🌐 www.simplyglin.com

📷 Instagram @simplyglin

in www.linkedin.com/in/glin-bayley-358b4514/